I0393949

Credit Card Management For The Single Daddy

Managing Credit Card Debt Effectively And Reduce Stress In Your Life

Nick Thomas

Visit my website at www.singledaddydating.com

ISBN-13: 978-1505405507

ISBN-10: 1505405505

JOIN OUR COMMUNITY!

Single Daddy Dating is a growing community of single fathers who look to help each other, not only with dating success but in all areas of their lives too. This includes parenting, career and finances advice.

Join us today and get '**10 Crucial Checklist To Dating Success For Single Fathers**' completely FREE!

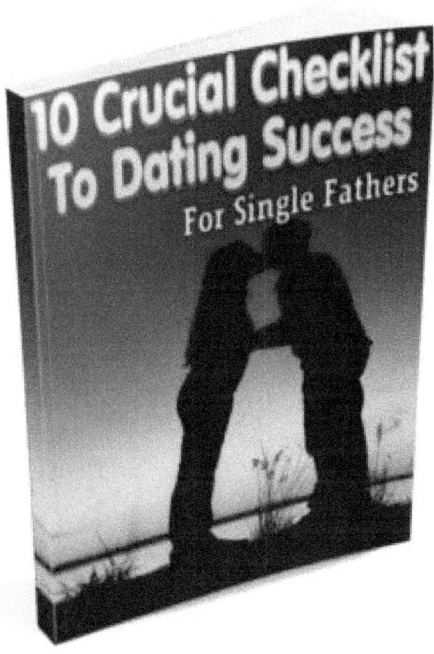

JOIN US AT

www.singledaddydating.com

CONTENTS

Chapter 1: The Credit Card Danger

One of society's biggest danger is the credit card. Over the past few years, I have seen many people who are crippled by credit card debt. Credit cards have this magical power of taking over a person's life due to its relative ease.

I have seen many young people being crippled with the misery of debt after they get their credit cards. If you walk around any university, you find that many of them have booths where they sign up college student for credit cards. Even at a young age, they have been crippled with this ease. This ease only makes life more difficult. Having a credit card can be a convenient thing, but it comes with a price. A big, big price.

Consumer debt has been rising each year. Everyone loves the ease of credit cards because it means that they don't have to pay for something straight away. We can wait and pay towards the 'end of the month'. However, come end of the month, few of us actually pay the total amount which we owe.

Credit card is extremely dangerous because it can become a habit. Due to credit cards, many people find it hard to control their spending. They splurge on whatever they see and want due to this ease.

"Sign and forget" they say.

This is especially for many single fathers I know of. There are single fathers I know who are crippled with debt because of their lack of control. There are various reasons for their excessive spending, but it is normally due to a lack of discipline.

Are you one of those single fathers who have problems with the use of credit cards?

If such, you need to do something. Don't put yourself in a spiral of debt that would only be more difficult in the future. The moment the bad habit becomes a habit in you, it would be harder to change.

From statistics, it has been known that three quarters of single fathers are using credit card debt to pay for their monthly expenses. Besides that, more than half of single parents owe money on the household bills.

That's the danger of credit card debt. You would end up owing a lot and wouldn't know how to manage. Because of the use of credit cards, many single fathers would also end up being stressed from having banks and other lenders pressuring them to pay up. It can be very tough when the banks keep on calling to request payment.

When you are stressed, you would struggle to be a proper single father. Being a single father, you want to be the best that you can. You want to have time for your children while providing the very best for your family.

Therefore the management of your credit card is very important.

In this book, you would learn about the management of your credit card debt. You would understand better what makes you use your credit cards excessively and what you can do to deal with it. You would see how you spend money based on emotional triggers and learn how to establish more discipline in your spending.

Simply put, you would learn how to control your credit card spending. You could also decide if you would want to completely eliminate credit cards from your life and the ultimate benefits of a lifestyle change.

Chapter 2: How Single Fathers Often Misuse Credit Cards

The management of credit cards is more often something emotional rather than logical. This is often the reason why many single fathers get into excessive amount of credit card debt in the immediate year after the divorce. Finding it hard to deal with the emotional intricacies of the divorce, they take the easy way out of spending excessively.

There is a widespread of single parent debt in

the USA at present. Due to the high number of divorce (some experts suggest it's 50% of all marriages), single parent debt has also been on the rise. The first factor that brings about this debt is due to the high cost of divorce.

The cost of divorce is high. This doesn't only factor the cost of hiring a lawyer but also the effects of it. After a divorce, a single father might find himself needing to pay alimony and child support. He would also need to pay for his own place of stay, if the court decides he need to move out.

This is the case for Richard from Los Angeles.

From his divorce proceedings, it was decided that he would need to pay alimony and child support. Added to it the mortgage on the house which his ex-wife and children are staying in, it adds up to a very high expense. He also need to consider his own needs such as rental for his new apartment and other living expenses.

Added up, he was in a dire position of living

on credit. Many single fathers are in such similar position.

The fact of the matter is that the law protects the woman more than the man in a divorce. Therefore, whenever a single father get a divorce, always be prepared to pay more than you expect. From experience, the only men who can deal with a divorce situation well are those who have been divorced a few times. They would have the experience to protect themselves and their assets.

After a divorce, a single father would tend to get emotional. These emotions makes him spend money. He would spend money to get over the feeling of abandonment and hurt. He may also spend money to win his children's heart. He may also want to give the very best to his children because of the guilt of splitting up with his ex-wife.

If he doesn't have the money, he would then put it on his 'plastic card', believing that he can easily pay it off in the future. His spending is to gain the validation from his children and to feel better about his situation.

But it doesn't end there.

In the future, a single father might also try to spend money to try to win over friends or dates. Because there is an emotional gap in his heart, he would try his best to fill it by the acceptance of others. I have seen single fathers go absolutely crazy when they spend money. They would be at bars and buy expensive bottles of wine to share with others. Some of these bill rake up to the thousands a single night.

Some single fathers try to take women out on dates and bring them to expensive places. They try to impress other people by these ways. Some even purchase expensive sports cars after a divorce, trying to obtain validation. I have known plenty of men who end up in huge credit card debts (or other debts) trying to attract women.

In summary, the following reasons are often

why single fathers misuse credit cards:-

- **Prove Themselves To Others.** They want to gain the validation of others through spending. They want to feel worthy.

- **Win Over Their Children.** Some single fathers look to buy an obscene amount of things for their children to try win them over during the divorce proceeding. Top on the list are gadgets. This is especially when the custody battle becomes intense and the children's opinions become important.

- **Forget About The Divorce.** Some men want to drown their sorrow by spending a lot of money. Some single fathers would spend plenty of time in bars or clubs looking to drink. Some pick up a huge amount of debt from drinking alone. They would buy other people drinks because they wouldn't want to be alone.

For single fathers, it can be a very lonely and depressed period when they are just after a divorce. They won't know what to do and having a credit card simply puts them in a financially critical position. If they don't know how to deal with their emotions well, they would end up in a big pile of debt before they even know it.

As a single father, I know the challenges. However, I hope you can control your finances even if it is difficult.

In the next chapter, you would learn about the potential benefits of using credit cards. From understanding the benefits of credit cards, you would be better off knowing when to use and when not to use credit cards.

Chapter 3: Benefits Of Using Credit Cards

Personally, I hate credit cards. I hate it like a burning rage because it puts me in a jail cell. I hate that it forces me to work in a job I hate to buy things I don't need to impress the people I don't care about.

But, this chapter is all about the BENEFITS of using credit cards.

The reason for this is because as you understand the real benefits of using credit cards, you would learn to understand how you can use it for its benefits rather than its disadvantages. When you start to understand how beneficial credit cards are, you would slowly learn to develop the right habits and attitude towards credit cards use.

Among the various benefits of using credit cards include:-

- **Ease Of Use.** Credit cards are easier than cash because you wouldn't need to store so much money in your wallet. You only need to take one credit card out and you don't have to worry. Being a runner, I love using it. If I go out for a run, I normally carry along my credit card instead of cash. If I carry cash, my sweat would normally make the money wet while having credit cards is easy. Simply place the credit card in the pocket and I'm ready to go. If I have to buy a drink on the road, I can simply use my credit card.

- **Safer.** If someone robs you, they wouldn't

ask for your credit cards. They would insist on the cash that you have. A robber that decides to take your credit card instead of cash is plain stupid. If you get robbed, simply call the credit card company immediately to cancel the card. As simple as that. That's the reason why credit card can be safer, most of the time.

- **Track Expenses Better.** It is much easier to track expenses on your credit card statement than having to write down whatever you spend (if you pay in cash). When you put everything on your card, you simply get a monthly statement that has a list of whatever you have spent throughout the month.

- **Better Cash Management.** There are some credit cards that give you zero interest when you purchase something. Although this is something that can be dangerous for some people, I have used this well. This zero interest means you buy something and pay in instalment at zero interest. I have used this to purchase electronic products that I need for work. If my computer costs $1000, it would be better to pay it using a zero interest scheme. If I pay in cash, I would be off by $1000 on the onset while if I pay using the scheme, I would be able to slowly pay it off each month. This allows me to have more cash to run.

Despite its various benefits, credit cards can be something dangerous if you don't use it well. You still need to establish firm discipline in using them. If not, you simply dig yourself a deep hole.

For example, although using zero interest scheme can be helpful, it can be fatal if you purchase excessively. Don't get into this thinking that just because you are paying zero interest, you should purchase multiple electronic products. There are some people who think this way. Just because you can make the minimum payment doesn't mean that you should buy everything you can.

However, understanding those benefits go a long way towards establishing discipline in your life. As much as I hate credit cards, I realize how beneficial it can be for my life. After understanding the benefits, I made it a point to establish discipline in my credit card use. I hope you understand the importance of discipline too.

Chapter 4: Establishing Discipline In Your Credit Card Use

From the previous chapter, I hope you have understood the importance of discipline in the use of your credit cards. Without this discipline, it would be better if you don't use credit cards at all. Simply open up your wallet, take out those credit cards and cut it off one by one.

Using credit cards with care means

understanding what you should and shouldn't spend on. Credit cards are meant for safety and convenience; not indulgence. It isn't a tool for you to show off to others by buying an excessive amount of things.

The number one rule of credit card management is: **Pay it off by the end of each month. Never allow the banks to charge ANY interest.**

As long as you follow this one rule, you are safe. You are allowed to use credit cards.

It has been said that one of the greatest wonders in the world is the power of compound interest. Many people, without realizing, allow their credit card debt to grow and together with it, the interest. When the interest accrues, the debt becomes harder to manage.

Take time to go through your credit card statement. Look carefully at how the interest is calculated (if you have interest due). See how scary it can be. That's the main reason why you shouldn't accrue any interest.

For many people, the thought of not having any interest on their credit cards may be completely unimaginable. They have been using it so much for convenience that it can be unfathomable for them to live without the interest. If you are one of them, you need to start to manage your debt first.

You need to control your debt to such an extend where you don't add to the debt. You need to take time to understand how your credit card works and ensure that you stop paying interest once and for all. In the next month, you need to pay the amount required so that no interest would be charged on your credit card. Make it a MUST-DO goal for the next month.

In the future, I even recommend having a plan to completely eliminate all debt and live a debt-free lifestyle. It is possible. You need to take baby steps to start this. Imagine living in a debt-free lifestyle. You wouldn't worry about making the credit card payments but can spend your time enjoying life.

Creating a plan to eliminate debt isn't that difficult. It can be hard initially, but once you develop the right habits, it becomes much easier. The steps to eliminate debt from your life would be the following:-

- **Stop Buying Things.** How can you expect to eliminate debt if you are constantly adding to the debt? You need to stop buying things that you don't need, once and for all. If you continue buying those things, it would be counter-productive to your plan. Think of buying things you don't need as digging a deeper hole for yourself.

- **Establish Your Debt Number.** How much do you owe the credit card companies? Check all your credit card statement and get a total. If you owe multiple credit cards, make sure you get the right information. This includes the minimum monthly payment and interest rate.

- **Create A Debt Repayment Plan.** After getting the debt number, you need to create a plan to repay the debt. Pay in such a way that you don't accrue any interest on the credit cards. If you really can't, try to keep the interest to a bare minimum.

- **Automate It.** After you have created a plan, make sure you automate it. Set up a standing order on your bank account to repay the amount at the beginning of each week/month, the moment your salary comes into your bank account.

- **Simplify Life.** Nothing is more important. If you don't simplify your life and focus on the essentials, you would end up constantly in this cycle of buying things you don't need. As a single father, you need to have a long term plan for your money. Think of the financial goals you have for your money and spend time planning for them.

Even if you have completely eliminated debt from your credit card, you need to have the right habits. The next important rule towards spending on your credit card would be:

Don't spend on your credit card if you can't pay it off towards the month end.

This discipline would mean that you never buy something that you can never afford in the first place. For now, it may seem like a long stretch for you (if you still have plenty of credit card debt). Give it time. Once you eliminate your debt completely, you can then develop this important habit.

Chapter 5: How To Manage Credit Card Debt

In the previous chapter, I have mentioned about the importance of establishing discipline in your credit card use. The moment you have got a grasp on the discipline required, you are safe to use your credit card. You should internalize this discipline, and the main way to do this is to…

Remind yourself all the time about the pain of having debt.

Whenever I think of debt, I think of the

things that I miss in life. I think of the children's recitals that I miss, the soccer matches and how I miss my children growing up. The pain of missing out on such things gives me the motivation to be disciplined with my debt, especially credit card debt.

In this chapter, you would find multiple tips that you can use to manage credit card debt. These are all valuable tips that can apply to your credit card management, one way or another.

(1) Know Your Credit History

The credit card interest rate and credit limit depends on your credit history. Surprisingly, many people don't know how good or bad their credit is. To obtain your credit history, get a credit report from a few credit reporting agencies. Ideally, get it from three agencies.

At AnnualCreditReport.com, you can pull a

free credit report from each agency annually.

This report has a detailed information of your account history and factors that would hurt your credit. This includes bad payment habits, short credit history of high utilization. The more negatives you have, the lower your credit rating. Thus, the higher the interest rates you need to pay.

(2) Understand The Benefits That You Want

You find that you have good credit history and now want a credit card, what do you do now then? You need to figure out the benefits that you want.

If you are someone who travels frequently, you would want a card that has association with hotels or airlines and allows you to rack up reward points. These reward points can be used to buy flights or hotel stays.

If you are someone who spends the credit card mostly on gas payments, there are several gas rewards cards available. If you are someone who wants cash back from your purchases, issuers have several types of cash back reward cards. There are also other forms of rewards such as cards with no balance transfer fees or certain specialty cards with low penalty fees.

(3) Compare Credit Cards

There are various things you need to check in the process of getting a credit card. It is sometimes shocking how some single fathers get credit cards simply because they are eligible too.

They don't check the fees they need to pay and the amount of interest rate they are eligible for.

Would the card cover annual fees?

How much is the Annual Percentage Rate (APR)?

Is there a low introductory rate and then shoots up later?

The card with the lowest APR isn't necessarily the best. You need to take into account the late penalty fees, especially if you are known to always miss payments. This is how the issuers make your money – by the penalties.

You also need to check other fees such as balance transfer fees and foreign transaction fees. These fees can be very high if you intend to use those benefits in the future.

(4) Other Perks

Credit cards come with other perks other than their rewards program. As a single father, you would want to benefit from perks because they can save you some money.

Among the perks include travel assistance,

purchase protection and roadside assistance. Check with the issuer to see if they do provide such benefits.

(5) A Bad Credit

There are some single fathers who have credit so poor that they wouldn't qualify for a credit card. If you are one of these people, you have two choices. You can either apply for a secured credit card or become an authorized user on someone else's card.

Secured credit card requires a deposit. This would be normally around $300 to $500. It works as a collateral. This deposit is put into a savings account, money market account or certificate of deposit. After a good year of payment, the issuer may turn the secured card into a regular card.

Being an authorized user on someone's card means to piggybank on someone's credit card like a spouse or parent. They add you as an authorized user without the need to qualify you.

(6) Have A Good Track Record

It may seem easy to pay just the minimum each month because there would be less money out of your pocket. However, you need to think about the APR. Even at 13%, you are paying a bucket load of interest. Paying the minimum payment would only increase what you owe.

There's when the rule comes into play…

Only charge to your credit card what you can comfortable pay off each month.

You also need to pay off on time, all the time. This prompt payment impacts your credit score severely. The other factor is to beware of your credit limit. If you utilize too much of your credit limit, it would also impact your credit score. The utilization of your credit limit is calculated as your utilization rate.

(7) Be Virtual Friends With Credit Cards

Credit card issuers are taking their credit cards services online. There would be special promotions on their Facebook page, Twitter and even Instagram. Look to 'like' or 'follow' their social media pages to gain the most out of your credit card.

Besides that, these issuers also give you news about complaints that would impact you. They use these social media to address certain customer complaints that might impact you. Even if they don't, it pays to know more about what is happening to these credit card companies.

(8) Keep A Good Tab

You need to make sure that your credit card is secured. You wouldn't want it to land on the wrong hands. Make sure that you store every credit card you have safely.

To do this, you need to monitor them properly. These are some tips that can help ensure your credit cards aren't use for fraudulent purposes:-

- Monitor the credit card accounts regularly. You can do this online. Make sure you understand every single transaction that is charged into the account.

- Don't make online purchases on public computers. Public computers are normally vulnerable to hackers.

- Never give your credit card information over the phone.

- Never purchase anything online from unfamiliar online vendors.

***

These eight tips are important because they ensure the safety of your credit cards. It makes sure that you are spending on the right things and that other people won't use it. You also need to keep a good eye on your credit score all the time.

Establishing good credit card habits go a long way towards using your credit cards properly. If you don't use it well, then it might be best if you...

ELIMINATE IT!

Should or shouldn't you eliminate it?

Chapter 6: Should You Eliminate Your Credit Card

Eliminating your credit card…

Can you ever imagine that?

Trust me, most people have a hard time imagining that ever happening in life. The convenience of having a credit card can be too much to ever imagine not having debt in their lives. If you are one of those people who have zero debt on their credit cards, perhaps you could still keep it.

In Chapter 3 – Benefits Of Using Credit

Cards, I have mentioned the incredible usage of credit cards. They are great tools for convenience and safety. But for some people, it is hell waiting to happen.

If you are one of those people who have trouble dealing with discipline with credit card use, perhaps the best way is to simply eliminate credit cards once and for all. Simply cut off all your credit cards. You don't have to do it immediately, but look to pay off your credit card debt and then cut them off in the future. Simply eliminate it.

The key question would be: Would it be feasible for you?

How would your life change without having a credit card?

Discipline is something that is elusive for some people. For these group of people, credit cards should be eliminated.

Think about how much you spend from your credit card. Take the records from a few months and see if you are really spending on things which are important. Go through every detail and put a tick on those items which aren't important. Be mindful about it the next time when you spend.

After a month, check through your previous month spending on your credit card statement again. See if you are still spending unnecessarily on those things. If you find yourself spending on the same unnecessary items, it may be an indication that you have trouble with discipline. Therefore, eliminating your credit card can be a wise choice.

If you are disciplined, you would find that your spending on those items would drop drastically. You can pay extra on reducing your credit card debt and look to save more money. Check the following to see if you are someone who is disciplined with credit cards:-

- **Do You Spend More Than 20% Of Your Monthly Income On Your Credit Card?** If you spend more than 20% of your monthly income, you need to stop using credit cards. This is my measure of excessive credit card usage. To establish disciplined credit card habits, you need to be charge to your card only what you can actually pay towards the end of the month.

- **Do You Use Your Credit Card To Spend On Necessary Or Unnecessary Items?** As you go through each item on your credit card statement, you should be able to easily gauge whether you are spending on necessary or unnecessary items. If you spend too much money on unnecessary items, eliminate the card.

- **How Much Interest Are You Paying Each Month On Credit Cards?** Are you accruing a lot of interest each month? This is an indication that you should eliminate the card. In the previous chapters, I have mentioned about not paying any interests whatsoever. If you are constantly paying interest on your debt, eliminate the card.

- **Is The Total Of Your Credit Card Debt More Than Your Annual Salary?** How much do you make a year? If your credit card debt is more than your annual income, immediately eliminate your credit card. This means that you are too dependent on your credit card already.

Eliminating your credit card doesn't have to be a drastic process. It might seem like a drastic one, but you still need to make it a gradual process. Learn to take time in developing the right credit card habits. If you find it hard to develop these habits, then only choose the drastic route.

There are many times where real change can only come by drastic measures. This may be one of them.

Chapter 7: Tips For Reducing Credit Card Debt

In the previous few chapters, I have mentioned about the steps to manage your credit card debt. In this chapter, I would guide you specifically on the steps to reduce your credit card debt.

This is great for those people who have a mountain of debt and don't know where to start. Too much debt and too little savings can be a tough situation for a single father.

A big percentage of single fathers rely on

credit cards to make ends meet. However, they don't need to be dependent if they know the steps to reduce their credit card debt first. This is an easy four-step process that any single father can take to reduce their credit card debt.

Step 1: Trim The Fat

This first step is the most important for anyone having problems with credit cards. This is especially for single fathers. Single fathers would wonder if their children's quality of life would drop if they suddenly reduce the expenses. However, this is necessary. You need to communicate to them about the importance.

Cut down on those unnecessary expenses such as TV subscriptions, magazine subscriptions, entertainment and other expenses that you don't need. If you find it hard to cut it out, go for the cheaper option. If you normally send your child for day-care, consider a cheaper option.

When you go for the cheaper options, tell yourself that it is only for a few months while you pay off the debt. There are other cheaper options for everything you spend on. Instead of having cable TV, you can stream movies online. If you spend a lot of money on magazine subscriptions, consider going to the library to read. Downsize as much as possible. Think of it as a few months of sacrifice for a new lease of freedom in the future.

Step 2: Budget

The moment you decide on where you can cut expenses and free up additional money, you need to create a monthly budget. Write down all your bill and expenses. Make sure you have a 'priority list' – this represents the expenses that are the main priority.

Be sure to keep your budget on track. It may take a few months to adjust to such a lifestyle, but you need to think of the long term. Once your children are comfortable, it would be much easier. Make them a part of your budgeting process and it would be easier for them to adapt to the change. Tell them about the reasons for the changes.

This shows them respect. It would make them feel more accepting towards the change in their lifestyle.

Step 3: Create An Emergency Fund

Once you have create a habit of paying off the credit card debt and not accrue any interest, you need to put the extra money from the budget into an emergency savings fund. This is money that you would use in place of credit cards should there be an emergency expense needed.

Many single fathers tend to use their credit cards for emergency. This becomes a bad habit as it would only increase the amount of credit card debt. Having this emergency fund ensures that you don't increase the interest amount.

There are some personal finance guru that encourage you to have this emergency fund before you start paying off the debt and I agree with them. Ideally, you should have around $2500 before you start to pay off the debt consistently. This amount helps to cover any sudden health expenses and repairs needed.

Step 4: Start A Debt Snowball

Once you have an emergency fund build up

that makes you secure, it is time to focus COMPLETELY on eliminating debt from your life. This is done through a 'debt snowball'.

A 'debt snowball' is when you add the amount you have been putting into savings to the minimum payment of your smallest debt.

The moment that debt is paid off, you would need to add that entire monthly payment amount to the minimum payment of your next smallest debt, and so on. Do this until all the debts are paid off. This process is known as debt snowball – you focus on the small debt first because it gives you the motivation to pay off the other ones.

Remember, the sooner you pay off the debts, the sooner you would have money to save for yours and your children's future.

***

This four-step process to reducing credit card

debt is a very simplified version for single parents. You would need to be disciplined to execute it. Ideally, you want your children to be a big part of this process as it would impact their lifestyles.

Chapter 8: Building Up Your Credit As A Single Father

If being a parent is difficult, wait till you have to be a single father.

The single fathers I meet often lament that being a single father isn't twice more difficult than being a father. It is TEN TIMES more difficult. Between being at work and parenting, it may seem like there never is enough time, money or energy. And the feeling may extent to your credit rating too.

You would barely have the time to check your

credit, much less fix it. Always remember this: When you are a single parent, you are always poorer than being a 'normal' parent.

Due to this, the pressure to have good credit is huge. You need to ensure that you have proper credit to purchase certain items with your credit cards. In this chapter, you would learn about ways to maintain and build your credit as a single father.

These tips would help you build credit as a single father:-

- **Get Credit Report And Credit Scores.** In Chapter 5 – How To Manage Credit Card Debt, I mentioned about a valuable resource – AnnualCreditReport.com. This is a wonderful resource that you can use to get free credit reports. After that, head to Credit.com. Sign up for a free account to get your credit scores updated monthly. Review your credit reports and credit scores carefully. If you find any mistakes, you need to dispute them.

- **Debt Consolidation.** While a consolidation loan doesn't solve the credit problem of expenses that exceed income, it would help simplify your life. You can do this by consolidation multiple debts into one personal loan. It would save you time and money. What this concept means is that you take a personal loan to cover all the credit card debts. From there, you only need to pay off the personal loan.

- **The Right Card Is Important.** If you still decide to have a credit card, you need to use the right cards together with the benefits that suit you. Probably you have decided to use a certain credit card because there are cashback benefits. You need to use the right one. Using the wrong one would only be counterproductive towards your goal of managing your credit card better.

Being a single father isn't always a bad thing. I have found that it can be great managing finances as a single father. You are completely responsible of your own financial future. You have full control over it, unlike when you are married and your ex-wife have a big say over what to spend.

Chapter 9: Why Minimalism

The minimalist movement has been gaining ground in recent years. Due to the increase in consumer debt, many people are looking to reduce their debt. This doesn't only mean credit card debt, but housing mortgage and car loan as well. They want to completely eliminate debt in their lives.

The minimalist movement is the ultimate in downsizing. The followers of this movement choose to live according to what they need. They are focused on the essential in life and what's important to them. It may be a passion or what's their priorities.

Jack from New Zealand is the one who introduced me the value of minimalism. He doesn't have a mortgage, car or even credit cards. He choose to live in a caravan which he built himself. It is called a 'tiny home'. The 'tiny home' movement is picking up speed. People around the world are choosing to build their own homes and not take on a mortgage which takes 20 years to pay off.

For many of us, we have allowed clutter to burden our lives. We have forgotten the things which are important to us. We spend our time collecting things that aren't important, only to realize that we have a mountain of debt. We end up with too many things.

This is the main reason for credit card debt. We don't have a focus in our lives. We have no idea what's important for us anymore.

Ask yourself: *What are the things which are important to you? What holds meaning to you?*

Minimalism is relative. For some people, minimalism means taking it to more extreme means. They live on a backpack and travel. For some, it has become a lifestyle so they could focus on doing something they love. Some have chosen to focus on building a business or writing books; while living a minimalist life.

They don't have to be in the rat race where they are constantly be on the chase for something. Simply put, they focus on what's essential to their lives and happiness.

Having the minimalist mindset can be important in the process of reducing your credit card debt. You can choose to live a minimalist lifestyle for a period of time while you eliminate your credit card debt.

Embracing this minimalist lifestyle after that

can also help you live happily. You would find that your life becomes more purposeful and you would have better control over all areas of your life.

Credit card debts can be managed, even if you are a single father with plenty of expenses. You simply need to focus. Minimalism is one way to give you that laser-like focus. Choose to embrace it and you would be able to reduce your debt easily.

LEAVE A REVIEW

I hope this book has helped you well. It isn't my intention at all to go deep into the topic. I am no expert in everything. However, I have the help of many other single fathers who have shared with me their invaluable experience.

If this book has helped you in any way, do leave me a review. This helps build our single father community.

If you feel that this book can be improved in any way, do mention it in the review. I would love to hear from you.

I wish you luck as a single father…

ABOUT NICK THOMAS

Nicholas Thomas has helped many single fathers cope with divorce in the past few years. By helping them gain more confidence and stability in their lives, he is able to guide them towards being a man that attracts other women easily.

He divorced back in 2008 and knows how difficult a divorce can be for a man. It was a terrible time for him when he got his divorce. He envisioned his children blaming him and not being able to spend time with him. It gave him a constant guilt trip.

Being a divorced man can be very difficult. Ever since his 'emotional recovery' from the divorce, he has helped many single fathers by advising and helping them gain confidence.

Should you want to share your story with him, you can do so at
www.singledaddydating.com/shareastory/

ALSO BY NICK THOMAS

(1) Dating After Divorce For The Single Daddy

(2) Dating Ideas For The Single Daddy

(3) How To Be An Alpha Male

(4) First Date Conversations

(5) Online Dating

(6) How To Approach Women

(7) Mature Dating

(8) Single Parent Support

(9) Coping With Divorce

(10) Parenting After Divorce

Visit www.singledaddydating.com/bookstore/

Get Your Complimentary
FREE BOOK

Join our community today and get **10 Crucial Checklist To Dating Success For Single Fathers** FREE, delivered right to your email…

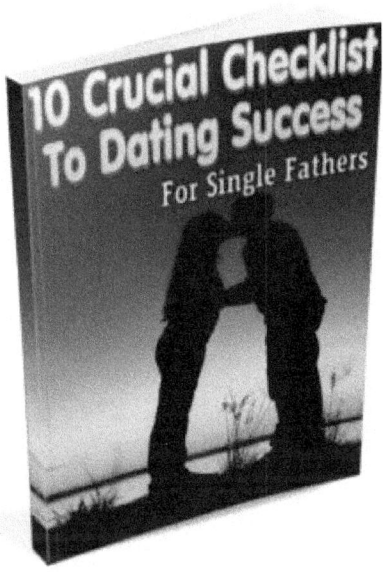

JOIN US AT
WWW.SINGLEDADDYDATING.COM/ NEWSLETTER/